D0403484

THE LITTLE BOOK OF
HUGS

THE LITTLE BOOK OF
HUGS

Lois Blyth

A gift to bring comfort and joy

CICO BOOKS
LONDON NEW YORK

Published in 2013 by CICO Books
An imprint of Ryland Peters and Small Ltd
20-21 Jockey's Fields   519 Broadway, 5th Floor
London WC1R 4BW   New York, NY 10012

www.cicobooks.com
10 9 8 7 6 5 4 3 2 1

A CIP catalog record for this book is available from the Library of Congress and
the British Library

ISBN: 978 1 908862 83 9

Printed in China
Editor: Ingrid Court-Jones
Designer: David Fordham

For digital editions, visit
www.cicobooks.com/apps.php

"I've learned that every day you should reach out and touch someone. People love a warm hug, or just a friendly pat on the back."

MAYA ANGELOU

What is a hug?

"To clasp or hold closely, especially in the arms, as in affection; embrace."

THIS IS THE DEFINITION OF A HUG FROM THE AMERICAN HERITAGE DICTIONARY OF THE ENGLISH LANGUAGE, FOURTH EDITION.

The origins of the word *hug* are uncertain. It may derive from the Old Norse *hugga*, which means "to soothe" or "to console;" this word is similar to the Old English word *hogian*, meaning "to care for."

A hug can make everything in the world seem right.

It doesn't matter what language you say it in—tell the world

Jag behöver en kram	Ich brauche eine Umarmung
Potrzebuję uścisk	Necesito un abrazo
Rabim objem	Muszę się przytulić
Eu preciso de um abraço	Jeg har brug for et kram
Ho bisogno di un abbraccio	Vennem kell egy ölelés
J'ai besoin d'un câlin	Ik moet een knuffel
Мне нужно обнять	Jeg trenger en klem
Trebam zagrljaj	Tarvitsen halauksen

...I need a HUG!

This little book is a happy tribute to hugs of all kinds.

7

A Hug is Worth 1000 Words

The wonderful thing about hugs is that when you hug someone, or something, the energy embraces both of you—so it becomes unclear who started the hug or where it will end. You become the hug and the hug becomes you.

Hugs are a short-cut to care and comfort. If someone is distressed, they may not feel like talking. A warm and comforting embrace provides a safe place to cry, to feel safe and cared for—without the need for words.

Hugs can say so much more than words, more quickly, and more warmly. There is very little room for misunderstanding when you are embraced wholeheartedly by someone who wants to communicate with you hug-wise.

"I love hugging. I wish I was an octopus, so I could hug ten people at a time."
DREW BARRYMORE, ACTOR

Love Across the Miles

"My husband is German; I am Italian. When we first met, we couldn't speak each other's languages and we lived in different countries, but we were determined to see each other as often as possible. For the first year our work commitments meant we spent very little time together and our language differences made it hard for us to talk or to write. As the months passed it felt as if a huge gulf was opening up between us. When I visited him at Christmas it was with a heavy heart because I knew I had to find a way to end the relationship. I was certain he was feeling the same way.

We spent a tense and over-polite first morning talking about nothing in particular. Finally I said, "We need to talk, don't we?" and burst into tears. With that, he looked at me with such love and held me in a close embrace until I had wept my heart out. I will always remember that feeling of total connection. Somehow that hug healed everything, without the need for words. We have been together ever since."

GIOVANNA, GERMANY

A Hug a Day Keeps the Doctor Away

What is it about human touch that makes it something we can't do without?

Experts say we need human touch 10 to 12 times a day. It may be the touch of a hand, a handshake, a tap on the shoulder, a stroke of the arm—or a hug.

Human beings are human animals; we need connection with others to make us feel alive.

So what is it about hugs that makes them so stress-relieving? When we're feeling low, getting a gentle squeeze provides comfort like nothing else. There are even therapeutic practices centered on hugging. When it comes to our health, the best thing we can do is open our arms.

Those who have worked in orphanages or with babies and infants who have been neglected, know that a lack of loving cuddles has a detrimental influence on the physical and mental development of small children. Any young child in institutional care who is

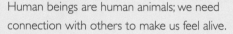

12

Hugs are good for our health. They make us feel loved, joyous, and alive.

deprived of love and cuddles is likely to become withdrawn, listless, and may suffer weight loss and slow growth.

Although humans are inherently social, many will shy away from physical contact—especially if they are feeling sad or lonely.

Compared to some other cultures, people in Western cultures tend to be very aware of personal space, offering a handshake instead of a kiss on the cheek, and keeping a certain distance between each other when engaging in conversation.

Unfortunately, keeping our distance is detrimental to our wellbeing. We need physical contact to feel connected to something other than ourselves and to feel a little less alone, especially in times of need. But when we're stressed or sad, we turn to a number of other coping mechanisms, such as eating comfort food or crashing out in front of the TV.

So the next time you are feeling down—don't turn to something that is bad for comfort—instead, reach out for a hug.

A Loving Hug is Good for the Heart

A medical study undertaken by a research team at the University of North Carolina studied the effects of hugging on men and women by monitoring 38 couples. Their blood pressure and their levels of cortisol (the stress hormone) and oxytocin (the "cuddle" hormone, a natural stress-buster) were measured both before and after the experiment.

During the experiment, couples relived a happy time in their relationship, watched a romantic movie, talked, and were invited to hug one another.

Both men and women showed an increase in oxytocin levels after the hug; but for women there were additional stress-reducing effects: their blood pressure went down and their cortisol levels were also reduced.

*"We are each of us angels with only one wing,
and we can only fly by embracing one another."*

LUCRETIUS, ROMAN POET AND PHILOSOPHER

Facts about Hugging

A hug begins long before two people put their arms out to one another. Edward T. Hall was an American anthropologist who spent years studying the connection between how close people stand to one another and how this correlates to their level of intimacy. He called this area of study Proxemics, and his findings are fascinating. He discovered that the distances varied depending upon cultural and environmental influences, which impact on how we read each others' signals.

- ♡ THE HUG ZONE, used for embracing, touching, or whispering
      Close: less than 6in (15cm). Far: 6–18in (15–46cm)
- ♡ THE FRIENDS AND FAMILY ZONE,: 18in–4 feet (46cm–1.2m)
- ♡ THE SOCIAL ZONE: 4–12ft (1.2–3.7m)
- ♡ THE PUBLIC ZONE: 12–25ft (3.7–7.6m)

So the next time you want to hug someone and you think they are standing too far away to show any sign of interest—consider their cultural influences, too. Do they come from a family or a culture that hugs? Or is their culture naturally more reserved? Acknowledging such differences helps us understand one another better and brings us closer together—and into the Hug Zone!

How to Give Someone a Hug

Nothing could be simpler than giving (or receiving) a hug—especially if you don't give yourself time to think, and just hug spontaneously. A hug given in love or friendship feels like the most natural thing in the world.

Put someone you don't know very well at their ease by smiling, and keeping the hug very brief. If it is a "making-up" hug, the opposite applies. Pull the person close and hold them dear, so they understand you are sorry and that they mean the world to you.

Not everyone likes hugging however, and some people may find physical closeness quite alarming. So when in doubt, don't hug—but always offer the opportunity. Hugs are for everyone who wants them.

" *A hug is the shortest distance between friends.*"
ANON

Loving Hugs

There are as many ways to hug as there are people on the planet, but one of the most delicious sort of hugs is the loving hug—the kind of hug that says, "You are my world and I am yours—if only for this moment." All kinds of messages can be given from within the closeness of someone's arms. A

loving hug communicates the feelings between two people. It may say, "I'm attracted to you," "I love you," or just, "You're my friend. You're like a brother or sister to me." Loving hugs are for sharing too. Wherever there is a camera there will be people snuggling up for a hug. Loving hugs that are on show are bright eyed and smiling. They trigger other people to hug and smile. Loving hugs are for keeps.

There is another kind of loving hug too. It is the breaking-up or upset hug. The kind that says "I am sorry I have hurt you; please forgive me." But the memory of the full hug keeps the emotional connection strong.

When a Man Hugs a Woman

The way that a man hugs a woman will depend on many things: whether he and she are related, married, in love, or just good friends. The important thing is to keep on hugging, no matter what your mood or how long you have known each other—and especially if you are married.

Types of Man-to-woman Hug

1. WHEN THE WOMAN IS THE MAN'S MOTHER
This is likely to be a full-on embrace—unless they are estranged and do not get along.

2. WHEN THE WOMAN IS THE MAN'S SISTER, COUSIN, OR OTHER RELATIVE
This is typically a warm but fast embrace with big smiles and both arms around each other's shoulders.

3. WHEN THE WOMAN IS SOMEONE THE MAN DESIRES
The man is likely to take the lead and instinctively put his arms around her waist. It can be a hug of protection and affection, as well as a sign of attraction.

4. WHEN THE WOMAN IS OLDER OR UNRELATED TO THE MAN
The man leans down to kiss swiftly on one or both cheeks and may pat the woman on her hand. This may be a respectful and gentle hug.

There are as many kinds of hug as there are reasons to embrace. A hug can express so much more than words—each and every day. They are such an easy way to express love and appreciation—and the longer you have been together the more precious they are to give and receive.

Hugs for the Girls

Girl hugs are a friendship thing—they are an easy extension of saying hello. Girl hugs are a way of saying a passing "thank you" for being there. They are a shortcut to saying "It's so good to see you. You can count on me."

Women and girls are generally very relaxed about hugging each other. Some sisters and close friends hug each other spontaneously—because they know they are hugging someone who knows them inside out.

But not all girl hugs are friendship hugs. Sometimes they are just for show. Social hugs may be exaggerated and include air-kissing. They tell the world, "It's party time, I am having a great time—and you are my new best friend!"

A girl hug sends the message that "You are my friend; we understand each other—and I like having you in my world."

Man Hugs

Man hugs have had a tough ride. They have not always been a sign of friendship. In days gone by a man-to-man hug was an easy way to make sure your guest wasn't carrying a lethal weapon. But these days, man hugs tend to be a joyful, robust affair—often including back slapping, joking, and hand shaking.

In politics, they are a sign to the world that there is cooperation and understanding. Socially, they are for sharing drinks and stories, watching sport and celebrating goals. A typical man hug says, "I'm really pleased to see you, but let's not overdo the hug thing."

Not all men are comfortable with man hugs. In some instances, a handshake shake is the nearest to hugging that a man will ever get. So for those who are uncomfortable with giving man hugs, here are a few friendly tips:

STEP 1: Shake right hands firmly.

STEP 2: Keeping the right hands clasped, lean in and slap your friend/brother/ father/uncle on the back with your left hand, two or three times.

STEP 3: Step back and release the hands.

STEP 4: Look slightly relieved that's over.

♡ Baby Hugs

Babies cry out for hugs—sometimes literally—but more usually just because they are babies—and they are cute, vulnerable, often smiley, usually adorable, and always deserving of the utmost love, care, and affection.

When you hug a baby, you need to be gentle. Their bones are still soft and their skin is super-sensitive. Holding a baby in a gentle hug can be a moment of magic.

Bear Hugs

There are two kinds of bear hugs: the human kind we give each other when we just don't want to let go, and the kind we give to bears of the small, fluffy, cuddly kind.

A bear hug is an all-or-nothing hug. It is a "squeeze-till-you-can't-breathe" kind of hug. It takes you out of this world for a moment, to a timeless place of safety and belonging.

Whether bears in the wild feel the same way about bear hugs is hard to say. But it would be nice to think so.

Dog Hugs

There are few creatures more full of joy in life than a puppy wanting a cuddle or a dog that loves its owner, ready for a hug.

Dogs give affection unconditionally. Their tails wag, they bark their approval, and they will jump up for more attention (if you let them).

Some dogs are natural huggers. They will stand on their back paws and lean up with front paws at the ready. Others are more likely to think you meant to give them a tummy rub. Dogs and humans have different priorities.

Hugging someone else's dog before you have been formally introduced may be very unwise. Dogs are territorial and may mistake your attention for an attack.

But generally speaking a dog hug is warm and forgiving—possibly involving a smelly blast of dog breath and a wet, slobbery lick!

 "Happiness is a warm puppy."
CHARLES M. SCHULZ, AMERICAN CARTOONIST

Cat Hugs

Cats can be hard to hug, because they like to be in control. They will only ever do things on their terms.

There are lap cats that can't get enough of being hugged, stroked, and pampered. These cats are a walking bundle of purring fur. Other cats will be gone in a flash if you try to pick them up for a cuddle. No human is going to intrude on their independence!

Some cats become more huggable as they get older—when they are more used to human touch and contact. Generally a cat hug is warm and purry, though be prepared for the occasional yowl and scratch.

To hug a cat, try to get it to come to you. If it doesn't want to jump up, try lifting it by scooping it up, and supporting the front of its body. Never constrain its paws, and try to avoid its tummy. Hold gently rather than squeezing. It's all about comfort and stroking in a cat's world.

*"Hugging would be so much easier if we were all cats.
We could just saunter up to the person we liked, wrap
ourselves around them, and purr into their ear."*

LUISA, SPAIN.

Horse Hugs

Hugging a horse is not an everyday experience. Most horses prefer to be hugged only when they have been properly introduced. Hugging a horse when you are not a horsey person may not be a good plan. They have quite big teeth! But if you know and love horses, a horse hug is a very special hug indeed.

A warm-up hug for a horse is a simple nose hug. Rubbing a horse's nose while you put your head against their head will tell the horse that you mean them no harm and that you care for them.

Hugging a horse is easiest when you are riding it. Just lean down and hug your horse's neck with both hands. (But make sure you don't fall off!)

Most horses love to be groomed and looked after. What can be more natural than giving a horse a hug while you are talking to them, to show your appreciation?

Tree Hugs

Trees play an important role in many cultures and religions. Not only do trees sustain life by providing us with oxygen by day, they also have long associations with myths of fertility, rituals, and immortality.

Who can fail to be moved by the sight of a magnificent tree? They often appear to have faces looking out of their gnarled bark. It is no wonder that different trees and tree types are believed by many to have an energy, as well as healing powers.

Tree-huggers come in all shapes and sizes. They may be small people who want to climb them; animals who hug them while they search for food and habitat; or adults who either want to add to or tap into the tree's energy.

Hugging a tree is simple—just put your arms around its trunk. Offering love to a tree is like caring for any living thing: it is all about treating it with respect and care.

31

A Hug for Every Occasion

A hug is multi-lingual and multi-sensory, it bypasses the need for language.

A hug can say, "Hello." ♡ A hug can say, "You're safe." ♡ A hug can say, "I am so happy to see you." ♡ A hug can say, "I'm sorry." A hug can say, "I love you." ♡ A hug can say, "I'll miss you." ♡ A hug can say, "Goodbye."

Children are unlikely to hug each other on first greeting, but may well offer a spontaneous "hello" hug when they are sitting together watching television or playing.

As we grow, hugs change from a being purely about comfort to being a way of expressing a greeting in friendship, or as a sign of attraction.

Later in life hugs are a reminder of being cherished and cared for in older age; being part of a family; or being old friends.

Whatever the occasion, there is a hug to fit the bill—even if it is disguised as a handshake, an arm rub, a shoulder squeeze, or the wink of an eye.

The Hello Hug

Hello hugs make the world go round. They are an everyday greeting that offers the warmth of human touch alongside a cheery "Hi." Hello hugs vary from country to country and from age to stage in life.

In some European countries, South America, and areas of the Middle East, an embrace is a natural part of saying hello, but the hello hug is becoming more popular in Western cultures too. High school students are much more likely to greet each other with a hug than their parents' or grandparents' generation.

A hello hug between old friends could take any form—and in the case of men may well include back-slapping and joking.

Girls are more likely to combine a hello hug with a kiss on both cheeks; boys, on the other hand, are likely to slap each other on the back in a more manly fashion.

"A hug is like a boomerang. You get it back right away."

BIL KEANE, AMERICAN CARTOONIST

The Side-by-Side Hug

This is a friendly hug. Side-by-side hugs are given to those we already know and feel comfortable with. They show kinship, friendship, or intimacy.

A side-by-side hug is a sign of togetherness. A young couple in a park or somewhere in public can give each other a sideways hug that says "I love you" without it intruding on anyone else.

A parent gives a young child a side-by-side hug to keep them close and safe; it is the perfect hug for a bedtime story.

A teenager will accept a sideways hug without resisting, because it shows understanding and love. A side-by-side hug creates a connection between two people that shows quiet understanding. It has another advantage too—it can easily become a cuddle.

Sideways hugs are always good hugs because they draw people together, but they also allow them the freedom to move away easily, too.

The Romantic Hug

There is love, there is sex, and then there is romance. Romantic hugs are the stuff of 1940s black-and-white movies. They conjure up a setting of wine, roses, and candles; of long walks and picnics. They are declarations of love and togetherness, and underlying passions.

A romantic hug is an old fashioned embrace; it makes the woman feel cherished and the man feel protective. A romantic hug of the movie-star kind involves smoldering looks and softly spoken words, heads held cheek-to-cheek, and gazing off into the sunset. This kind of hug cannot be planned; it just happens. These are precious moments of love and intimacy. Everyone deserves to experience a romantic hug at some time in their lives.

> "The strength of a man isn't seen in the power of his arms. It's seen in the love with which he embraces you."
>
> STEVE MARABOLI, AUTHOR

Hug, Hug Me Do

If you are on your own, you can still have a great big hug—you can give a hug to yourself. Remember when you were a teenager, imagining that you would be swept away by the love of your life?

Most people have laughed at a friend pretending to have a smoochy hug with someone who is not there. But you don't have to give yourself a smoochy hug. Just wrap your arms around yourself and give your body a big, comfortable squeeze. If you're lying in bed you can use a pillow for extra cuddle comfort.

It's a great way to start or finish the day and gives your arm muscles a good stretch, too.

"You, yourself, as much as anybody in the entire universe, deserve your love and affection."

SIDDARTHA GUATAMA

The Story-Telling Hug

Children love seated hugs because they can quickly become a story-telling hug. A grown-up's lap can transform into a comfy chair in a moment—and there is nothing more secure than being wrapped in warm arms and being read your favorite story.

"Katherine sat with Benjamin on one side of her, Rebecca on the other and a book in her lap. All of a sudden a little voice spoke up. "What about me, me, me?" and a little head popped up beneath the book. Oliver had arrived and wanted to sit on Mummy's lap. Katherine looked across at Sebastian—not yet old enough to join them, but wide-eyed and gazing from his cot. The four of them sat, embraced in a big story-telling hug, as she read Winnie-the-Pooh for the umpteenth time."

SARAH, UK

The Knee Hug

Only a child can give a meaningful knee hug.

Imagine what it is like to be very small, in a sea of adult legs, where conversation is taking place far above your head—and you are bored, anxious, tired, feeling ignored, wanting attention, or all of the above.

Too small to reach up and put their arms around you, a child will clutch on, in a loving and needing way, to the one part of your body that they can hold on to—your leg. A knee hug is a clever move because in one instant it anchors you to the spot, while making the child feel safe—and hopefully it gains your attention.

Of course, if the child has grabbed on to a strong leg there is always the chance of a funny ride around the room, too. The hug becomes a "cling on" as the child is marched around in fun and glee. A knee hug says "I'm here too. Please don't forget about me."

"When we are young, we can't wait to grow up, and to embrace the world as adults do. But no matter how tall we grow, we will always remember how it felt to hug and be hugged as a child. It is when we are very small that we first learn that a hug can stop time and make everything better. A hug is as delicious as home-made candy— when one child is given some, everyone else wants some too."

INGRID, NORWAY

Grandparents Need Hugs, Too

There are few things in life more likely to melt a grown-up's heart than the sight of a young child rushing up for a hug and a cuddle—especially if that child is your grandchild. A grandchild's hug can make a grandparent feel instantly younger, loved, and loveable.

"My father led a very healthy and independent life well into his nineties; but then he suffered a series of strokes and spent quite a few weeks in hospital and in care. We were terribly worried because he no longer smiled and seemed to have lost the will to live. One day, when we couldn't get childcare, we took our toddler on to the ward with us. Far from being unnerved by the change in her granddad, she rushed up to him, gave him a big squeeze and began to chatter, non-stop. For the first time in ages his eyes lit up—and from that day forward he began to make more of an effort to recover. We took Stacey back in to see him as often as possible. There is no doubt in our minds that the healing power of her hugs set him back on the road to recovery."

JEMMA, UK

Group Hugs

The group hug is a party and festival hug. It is a sign of friendship and shared experience.

The Huddle

The group hug is not the same as a huddle. Huddles usually take place in sport. These are "man hugs." They show unity and bond the team together physically and mentally—so the sporting huddle is a group hug in preparation for competition. A team of people pulling together have more energy and power than one person on their own.

The Team Hug

This is similar to the sporting huddle, but it applies to any group of co-workers. It is a "musketeers'" huddle that cries out, "all for one and one for all!" Members of a team who hug each other work for each other, as well as for their company or business.

"Alone we can do so little, together we can do so much."
HELEN KELLER

The Comforter

We all need love and comfort from time to time, at every age and stage of life. The comforter is a soothing hug, the sort that a caring adult or sibling will offer as comfort to a baby or a little brother or sister, or that one friend will give another.

The comforter requires something soft and soothing to ease the pain and calm the soul.

Young babies and small children may take great comfort from hugging a cuddly toy, the cat, the dog, or a favorite comforter. They will often give themselves a comfort hug by holding a soft piece of cloth against their cheek or sucking a thumb.

Toddlers, teens, and many adults have a favorite teddy bear or other soft toy animal that offers comfort when times are bad or sad.

Pets are great comforters, too. They often know instinctively that something is not right and will offer furry comfort to their owners as if to say, "I am here. You are not alone."

"I have a tubby brown bear called Tobias. He was a 21st birthday present and is very precious. Tobias is very soft and has a large round tummy built for hugs. There have been times of heartbreak in my life when having a private sob and cuddling Tobias has helped me to regain my composure before facing the outside world. Somehow that large brown bundle is able to offer me comfort. Silly, isn't it?"

MAGDA, USA

The Farewell Hug

Farewell hugs are always given at a time of mixed emotions. They are memorable hugs that mark times of change and transition.

You may feel excited to be going away or sad, tearful, or anxious at someone's departure. Farewells make us aware that nothing is permanent and that our loved ones and our memories are very precious.

Giving your loved one an enormous squeeze can help you to get yourself under control—literally—as the pressure on your solar plexus will calm you down.

Farewell hugs are offered to remind the other person that you will be there for them, even though you or they are going away.

They are tough hugs, because they mark endings as well as new beginnings. There are only two guidelines for a farewell hug: Hug like you mean it and put on a brave face. A farewell hug is about being strong for the other person as well as sending a message.

A farewell hug may be remembered years after the person you said goodbye to has either returned or gone on to other things.

The Thank-You Hug

A thank-you hug is a lovely warm gesture that is as wonderful to give as to receive. A thank-you hug tells the person who is hugged how much they are loved and appreciated—not only for their gift or kindness, but for all they have offered in love and friendship.

Do you have an older person in your life? Do they live alone? Never miss an opportunity to give that person a thank-you hug, just to thank them for being there and playing a part in your existence.

Celebratory holidays, such as Christmas and birthdays are perfect occasions for thank-you hugs. Don't hold back, and make the most of them. But thank-you hugs are great for everyday, too.

The Healing Power of Love

Would you believe that people come from all over the world to get a hug from one woman from India? Amma, which means "mother" in Malayalam, has hugged well over twenty-five million people since she started traveling the globe and opening her arms to others. Amma believes in the healing power of love and its ability to transform people and their lives.

"Everyone has the power within, it just needs to be awakened," she says… "It is a God-given gift to every single person in this world. It's like an ember, you have to constantly blow on it and eventually it will become like a wild fire."

Amma is also known as the "hugging saint," and she donates her time and money to numerous charities.

Amma, the "Hugging Saint"

"How you receive the hug is more important than the amount—the contentment you feel when you receive it, that's most important."

Hugs by Post

There is nothing as comforting as a physical hug—but hugs can be sent virtually, too—by phone, by email, and by letter.

A wonderfully warm and loving letter; or words of love and tenderness by phone are the next best thing to having a real hug.

Words can reach out and touch the ones you love and stir the memory of what it was like to have you near.

"Michael is stationed overseas for much of the year. The kids and I miss him terribly—so we write, every day. The kids call it sending Dad his daily hug."

TRISHA, USA

Cuddle Workshops

Are you missing quality touch in your life?

Do you struggle when offered more than a handshake? Marcia Baczynski, Len Daley, and Dr Betty Martin are behind a hug movement in the United States known as cuddle parties. In their separate work as therapists they came to realize that there was nowhere for those who needed human comfort to go for a cuddle or to experience the

comfort of touch in a safe and non-sexual environment. Their carefully guided cuddle workshops help people to break down barriers and learn how to relate to one another.

The cuddle parties have created their own language. Cuddle party workshops end in a "cuddle pile."

The Rescuing Hug

In May 1966, an article called "A Sister's Helping Hand" appeared in *Reader's Digest*. It told the story of a staff nurse called Gayle Kasparian and her role in the lives of two tiny sisters who were born prematurely.

Kyrie and Brielle Jackson had been born on 17 October 1995, at the Medical Center of Central Massachusetts, 12 weeks ahead of their due date. In line with standard practice they had been placed in separate incubators to minimize any chance of infection.

Kyrie, at 2 lbs 3oz, was the larger of the two, and she began gaining weight and sleeping calmly. Brielle, however, developed breathing and heart problems. She weighed only 2 lbs at birth and she wasn't gaining weight quickly enough.

Four weeks later, on 12 November, Brielle became critically unstable. Her oxygen intake dropped, her heart rate soared. Nurse Kasparian tried everything in the book to save her. Then she recalled a technique used in Europe called "double-bedding", used for premature, multiple-birth babies. With the parents' permission and in desperation, she went against standard hospital practice in order to reunite the twin girls.

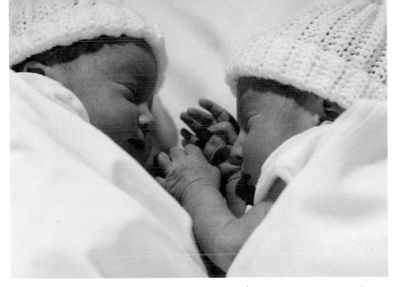

The story tells how, as soon as they were reunited,
Brielle snuggled up to Kyrie—and calmed down.
Within minutes her blood-oxygen readings improved.
As Brielle dozed, Kyrie wrapped her tiny arm around
her smaller sibling. Both babies survived and the
hospital adopted the policy as the new standard practice.

The World-Record Hug

In January 2012, six couples took part in a 24-hour "hug-a-thon," in the first of a series of record-breaking events organized by London & Partners ahead of the London Olympics. The couples met at St Pancras Station in central London at 7am beneath an iconic statue called the Meeting Place, featuring young lovers saying goodbye in a head-to-head hug.

In order to beat the Guinness World Record the couples needed to stay entwined for a minimum of 24 hours and 34 minutes. They had to stay awake throughout and could have a maximum of 5 minutes' break per hour.

Four of the six couples made it, setting a new record of 24 hours and 44 minutes.

The long embrace marked annual Hugging Day, on 21 January.

The Best Movie Hugs Ever

A survey in an American magazine asked readers to vote for their "Best Movie Hugs Ever." The top five were:

1. TITANIC—the iceberg strikes the Titanic, and Jack (Leonardo DiCaprio) gives Rose (Kate Winslet) a hug as the ship sinks.

2. DIRTY DANCING—the first embrace between Baby (Jennifer Gray) and Johnny (Patrick Swayze.)

3. E.T.—the moment when Elliot (Henry Thomas) hugs extra-terrestrial E.T. in the incubator.

4. BRIDGET JONES'S DIARY—Bridget (Renée Zellweger) runs after Mark Darcy (Colin Firth) in the snow, wearing only underwear and a cardigan.

5. THE SHAWSHANK REDEMPTION—the final scene, featuring ex-convicts Andy (Tim Robbins) and Red (Morgan Freeman.)

Other hugs that made the top ten included embraces in THE LION KING, IT'S A WONDERFUL LIFE, LOVE ACTUALLY, PRETTY WOMAN, and THE SNOWMAN.

Hugging Etiquette

The best sorts of hugs are warm, spontaneous, and given freely—but not all hugs are welcome or appropriate, so it is worth remembering a few basic rules of hugging etiquette.

♡ Always invite someone to have a hug, rather than assume they would like one—especially if you have never met before.

♡ If the person you are going to hug has their arms wide open and they are smiling, the chances are they won't mind being hugged. If they move backward when you make your move, or have their arms by their sides, stop! You are not being welcomed and are making them uncomfortable.

♡ Never confuse a family hug or a friendly hug with a lover's hug. You may cause distress or lose a friend.

♡ Saying yes to a friendly hug is not an agreement to an intimate kiss.

♡ Friendly hugs are short hugs, unless you know the person well.

♡ Don't assume that all cultural traditions are the same. In some countries hugging is an extension of saying hello; in other places there is a more reserved approach.